HOW TO CONVERT

TO ISLAM AND

BECOME MUSLIM

What You Need to Know, Believe, and Practice After Submitting to Your Creator

From The Sincere Seeker Collection

TABLE OF CONTENTS

WHAT IS ISLAM
IN A NUTSHELL?

Before we speak about converting to Islam and what you need to know and do after converting, let me quickly introduce Islam. Islam is defined as the voluntary act of submitting yourself to God. When you become a Muslim, you submit and surrender to the will of God, just as the creation around you, providing you peace and contentment in this life and the hereafter. Only when you submit to God, through a process of believing in Him and obeying His commandments, do you achieve an innate and lasting sense of security, true peace of mind, and surety of heart. As a Muslim, you don't live to fulfill your desires, lusts, and impulses; instead, by definition, a Muslim submits their will to the almighty God. You acknowledge and trust that God knows what's best for you, so you follow His guidance.

You cannot live peacefully or successfully without religion, and this religion cannot be man-made. Religion must be utterly Divine, with no human alteration inherent. The only Revelation in the world today that still rings good and true is the final Book, the last and final Testament of God, the Holy Quran. All other traditional Revelations have been lost in the annals of time or undergone endless human-made modifications that have rendered them impractical for humanity. Unlike other sacred

1

scriptures such as the Bible, the Holy Quran has been perfectly preserved in both its words and meaning—and in a language that still exists today.

Islam is a monotheistic faith that requires followers to admit and recognize the existence of one Supreme God and Being who is Almighty, All-Powerful, All-Knowledgeable, All-Seeing, All-Hearing, Most-Merciful, and Loving. Islam stresses the existence of only One God. The same God worshipped by Prophet Adam, Noah, Abraham, Joseph, Moses, David, Solomon, Jesus, and Prophet Muhammad, peace be upon them all. Islam demonstrates the fact that, through the centuries, God has continued to bless humanity with holy Prophets bearing the same general message.

The message is simple: you should worship God Alone with no partners, love Him with all of your heart, and follow His Commandments. If you follow this edict, you will live a content life in this world and enter Paradise eternally in the afterlife. If you do not believe in God and follow His commandments, you will live a depressed life and enter hellfire in the afterlife.

Islam is not a religion solely based on creeds, customs, and rituals such as praying and fasting; instead, Islam is a complete way of life that guides followers in every aspect of their lives. Islam teaches the art of living and dictates how you should steer and navigate your life. Islam instructs you about the things in this life that are beneficial to you and those that are ultimately destructive and should be avoided.

Islam states that everyday human acts, such as eating, drinking, greeting others, sitting, learning, dressing, sleeping, and giving charity, are all acts of worship if conducted for God alone and in accordance with His Divine Laws and guidelines.

WHO IS ALLAH?

And before we speak about converting to Islam and what you need to know and do after converting, let me quickly introduce your Creator to you. Muslims do not worship a particular God of Muslims; instead, the God that Muslims worship is the universal God who created the heavens and the Earth, which many people believe in from the time of their childhood. The word "Allah" is the unique name of God and translates to mean God. Regardless, some people harbor the mistaken belief that Muslims worship a different God than Christians and Jews do and that "Allah" is the God of the Arabs or the Muslims. This is far from the truth.

Arabic-speaking Jews and Christians use the same name, "Allah," to refer to God. If one were to examine an Arabic translation of the Bible, one would see the word "Allah" being used in place of the term, God. However, Muslims, Christians, and Jews have different concepts of God.

Allah is the one and only absolute and eternal God. He is the Creator of the Heavens and Earth, the Creator of the Universe. He is the Lord of all lords and King of all kings. He is the Most Compassionate and Most Merciful. Allah Neither Begets nor is He Begotten. And He knows no equal.

Say, "He is Allah, who is One, Allah, the Eternal Refuge. He neitherbegets nor is born, nor is there to Him any equivalent." (Quran 112:1-4)

Muslims believe in one unique, incomparable God—one with no son, daughter, father, mother, family, or partner. He is the Knower of the unseen and the Source of All Mercy. He is the Creator, the Maker, the Fashioner, the Wise. All that is in the Heavens and on Earth magnifies Him. Muslims believe that none should be worshipped but Him alone. He is the true God, and every other deity is false. None carries the right to be worshipped, revered, adored, invoked, supplicated, or shown any act of worship but Allah alone.

God is unique, indivisible, and similar to nothing. Whenever you try to compare God to anything in this world, the source of comparison cannot be God because God, to put it simply, is incomparable. Your finite human mind cannot comprehend and grasp God as a concept. Muslims avoid conceptualizing His image because imagining or visualizing Him would limit Him. The human imagination is limited, as it is based on what it observes and experiences directly. The human imagination cannot fully grasp God's state, which is timeless and eternal with no beginning or end. God has a unique nature and is free from gender and human weakness. He is beyond anything which human beings can imagine.

"There is no god but He, the Creator of all things; then worship Him, and He has the power to dispose of all affairs. No vision can grasp Him, but His grasp is over all vision; He is the Sublime, Well-Aware." (Quran 6: 102-103)

God is the King, the Holy, free from all defects, The Protector, the Keeper, the Sustainer of Earth and the Universe and all it contains. He is the Glorious, the Great, the deserver of all Praise. The Kingdom of the Heavens and the Earth belong to Him. Nothing is hidden from Him, and nothing is beyond His capabilities. He is the One that merges the night into the day and the day into the night. He is the Master of the Day of Judgment. Allah does not sleep nor slumber, nor does sleep overtake Him.

"He is Creator of the Heavens and the Earth. He has made for you from yourselves, mates, and among the cattle, mates; He multiplies you thereby. There is nothing like unto Him, and He is the Hearing, the Seeing." (Quran 42:11)

God is Loving, Compassionate, and Merciful; He is the answerer of prayers. He is indeed involved and concerned with the daily affairs of all human beings. God is the Beneficent, the Merciful. He is the Giver of life and the Causer of death. He is the Master of the Day of Judgment. He is the Most-High, the Most-Supreme.

God created all things from nothing. He does not need His creation, although His creation needs Him. He is all Knowledgeable and encompasses all things: the open and the secret, the public and the private. He knows all the secrets that lie hidden in the hearts and minds of men. He knows all that happened in the past, what is happening now, and what will happen in the future. Our Lord neither errs nor forgets. He is free from all defects and imperfections. He is the One that accepts repentance from His servants and forgives all sins. Allah knows what you endure and understands your feelings and struggles. Allah understands because He was there with you all along.

Allah has power over all things. No other power, might, strength, or influence can cause benefit or harm to anyone or anything except that which flows through Him. Nothing can happen unless God wills it so. God can make anything happen.

"Not a leaf falls but that He knows it. And no grain is there within the darkness of the earth and no moist or dry thing but that it is written in a clear record." (Quran 6:59)

**"Whenever We will anything to be,
We say unto it Our word "Be," and it is." (Quran 16:40)**

Some people assume that God is a harsh, stern, cruel God who demands to be respected, worshipped, and obeyed fully. They assume He is not loving and kind to His creation. Nothing could be further from the truth. God is All-Loving. He claims among His Names Al-Wadoud in Arabic (the Loving One). The love of God in the Holy Quran is expressed and emphasized many times throughout His Book. God bespeaks His love for the righteous, the charitable, the steadfast, the doers of good, the just, the fair, the benevolent, those who trust Him, the ones that are clean, the ones that purify themselves, and the ones who fulfill their obligations.

The entire Universe contains proof of Allah's love for all of His creation. God gives, without measure, to His servants. He gifted you with life and the ability to hear, feel, taste, and see. God gifted you your heart, mind, soul, strength, and skills. He loves you so much that He gave you an endless variety of foods to feast on, a vast array of land and wildlife, the sun, the moon, the stars, family, offspring, and much more. Everything you see, feel, hear, taste, and smell are blessings given to you by our Loving Creator. He didn't have to create these miracles, but He chose to bestow these blessings upon you. His boundless mercy encompasses everything.

**"And He gave you from all you asked of Him. And if you should count the favor of Allah, you could not enumerate them. Indeed, mankind is [generally] most unjust and ungrateful."
(Quran 14:34)**

God is also All-Just. Hence, evildoers and sinners must be held accountable for their actions. God is holy, righteous, and fair. If He didn't punish evil, He would allow that evil to exist without consequences. Since God cannot allow that to happen, His justice requires that a proper punishment be incurred and executed for evil sins. Although Allah is not answerable to anyone, He has promised to be Just and Fair to everyone.

He has prohibited injustice against the innocent. Allah never would punish an innocent person nor hold anyone accountable for the sins of another. Unlike Christianity, Islam imposes no burden on the original sin. Every human being is born with a clean slate and is rewarded or punished based only on one's willful intent, words, and deeds. Allah is the Absolute Judge, the Legislator. God is the One who distinguishes right from wrong. God even is more merciful to His creation than a mother is to her child. God is far removed from the blight of injustice and tyranny. He is All-Wise in all His actions and decrees.

When you genuinely ponder the Majesty of Allah, your humility increases. You are advised to study and ponder His Names and Attributes and are encouraged to worship and call Him by those names. God states:

"And to Allah belong the best names, so invoke Him by them." (Quran 7:180)

God is close to those who believe in Him and answers their every call. Nothing is hidden from Him regarding what His creation does or says. He knows all. Saying God is with His servants does not mean He intermingles or dwells with His creation; instead, He establishes His presence through His Knowledge and Power. God is above the heavens and above His Throne. God is outside of His creation. He never is contained by any physical dimension. God states in the Quran:

"Verily, Allah knows all the hidden things of the Heavens and the Earth; Verily He has full Knowledge of all that is in (men's) hearts." (Quran 35:38)

He sees and knows every aspect of His creations. He hears every word uttered. He is even knowledgeable of one's inner thoughts. God knows all of our dreams, secrets, desires, and wishes. Nothing is hidden from Him.

"We created man, and We know what his own self whispers to him. We are nearer to him than his jugular vein." (Quran 50:36)

Allah does not need you, although you do need Him. Allah wants you to worship Him for your own benefit. You need God in your life at all times and for every purpose. When you recognize the Majesty of the Creator of All, you will become awestruck and humble in your response. Rejecting God and His Guidance is like a patient refusing their doctor's medicine to remedy their pain. You will be foolish, ignorant, and illogical if you reject Allah. Allah is Fully Omnipotent and Self-sufficient. He is in no need of humanistic worship or anything else.

Allah is Perfect.

HOW DOES GOD
COMMUNICATE TO YOU?

Lastly, before we speak about converting to Islam and what you need to know and do after converting, let's quickly go over how our Creator communicates to His servants—to you and me. How would you know your role in life, your true-life purpose, unless you receive clear and practical instructions about God's wants and expectations of you? To glean this knowledge, we have a need for Prophethood and Revelation. God has sent thousands of Messengers and Prophets to humanity to convey His message and communicate with us. Every nation on Earth received a Prophet for this purpose. They all preached the same general message that only one deity is worthy of worship. He is the One and Only God, without a partner, son, daughter, or equal.

God sent Messengers and Prophets to guide humanity, to deter them from worshipping created beings in lieu of worshiping their Creator, the Creator of all things. The Prophets taught their people the identity of their Creator, how to build a relationship with Him, and how to love Him. The Prophets taught their people that life is only a test; those who pass will enter Paradise eternally, while those who fail will be subjected to the ultimate punishment in the afterlife.

As an extension of His mercy and love, God continued to send Messengers with Books to guide humanity, starting with Prophet Adam and including Noah, Abraham, Ishmael, Jacob, Moses, Jesus, and Prophet Muhammad, peace be upon them all. Many of the Prophets are mentioned in Jewish and Christian traditions. All previous Messengers and Books, other than the Holy Quran and Prophet Muhammad, peace be upon him, were sent only to those specific groups of people intended to receive the message and were meant to be followed only for a particular period.

For example, Prophet Jesus, peace be upon him, was one of God's mightiest Messengers, who was sent down with the same general message as the previous Prophets, but he was sent to speak to only the Children of Israel—the nation where he resided, that existed before us—as their final Prophet because they were disobeying the commandments of God and veering away from the laws sent down by the previous Messenger, Moses, peace be upon him.

Whenever God sent Messengers with Revelations, people would distort and change the Revelations after they were passed. What originated as pure Revelation from God would be polluted with the words of men, myths, superstitions, irrational philosophical ideologies, and idol worship. Just like how Prophet Jesus PBUH was sent to revise the previous message sent before him by the Messenger Moses PBUH, Prophet Muhammad PBUH came to reform Prophet Jesus' Message, as it had been distorted by his people and did not survive in its original form.

When humanity existed in the depth of the Dark Ages, God the Almighty sent his last and final Messenger to humankind—Prophet Muhamad, peace be upon him—and his final Revelation, the Holy Quran, to redeem humanity. The Holy Quran and the final Messenger affirmed everything revealed to the previous Messengers.

No Messenger or Prophet will come after him, nor will there be a Book released after the Holy Quran--since both are meant to be followed by all people living today until the end of time. The Holy Quran is God's Message to you, so read it. Prophet Muhammad PBUH is your Prophet, so you should obey and follow him. Obeying and following Prophet Muhammad PBUH equates to obeying and following God, the Almighty because God instructs you to follow the Prophet sent to you.

Contrary to popular belief, Islam is not a new religion that came into existence just 1,400 years ago, back in the 7th century. Islam has existed since the first moment that man set foot on the Earth. Throughout history, anyone who practiced monotheism by submitting to the will of God and following their Prophet was considered a Muslim. Human beings have been practicing Islam since the creation of Prophet Adam PBUH.

Islam is the only religion that God ever commanded humankind to follow. Islam, therefore, is the only religion that has ever been acceptable to and ordained by God. The final Prophet of humanity, Prophet Muhammad PBUH, was not the founder of Islam, as many people mistakenly believe. Instead, he was sent as the last and final Prophet— one delivered from the hand of Almighty God to convey His message to our nation, the final nation. Islam is the continuation, the culmination, and the completion of God's universal and eternal message to humanity, as revealed to all of God's previous Messengers and Prophets.

HOW DO YOU
CONVERT TO ISLAM?

You convert to Islam, embracing the fold because you chose to submit and surrender to the Will of your Creator voluntarily. You realize that you were created to worship God, and only when you submit to the one true God and live according to His Divinely revealed Laws will you achieve true peace of mind and surety of heart. You understand that no one is worthy of your worship and veneration except the One True Creator, the ultimate Creator, the Creator of this World, and everything in it. You realize that the only true purpose of your life is to find God, build a relationship with Him, and follow His commandments.

You realize that God, the Almighty, would not leave you in darkness without guiding and showing you how He wants you to live. So, your Creator chose Messengers and Prophets throughout history to send to different nations at different times to communicate His Message to humanity and show how you should live and to teach you about Him. These prophets came with glad tidings, stating that whoever Worships the One God with no partners and lives a righteous life while obeying God's commands will enter Paradise eternally, and whoever worships other than Allah and does not follow God's commandments will enter hellfire.

You convert to the faith, realizing that Islam will change your life for the better and that Islam will provide you the light to guide your life and grant you true salvation from eternal hellfire. You have searched for your life's purpose and your Creator, sincere and curious to learn the truth. Now you are being guided to the truth by the Will of God and by His Mercy, Love, and Justice. God decided to guide you. He guides those He Wills and Pleases.

You realize that Islam is the true religion of God, and you are ready to embrace the fold. In Islam, every action begins with an intention, so start by setting an intention in your heart to embrace Islam for the sake of God alone. It's highly recommended that you first take a bath or shower to symbolically purify and cleanse yourself of your past life and past sins. It's also recommended to wear suitable clothes on the day of your conversion.

Unlike other religions, converting to Islam does not involve rituals, ceremonials, or baptisms. All you have to do is declare the testimony of faith, known as the Shahada in Arabic, the first of the five pillars of Islam. These two statements encapsulate all the beliefs of Islam:

أشهد أن لا إله إلا الله وأشهد أن محمدا عبده ورسوله

'I bear witness that there is no deity worthy of worship except Allah, and I bear witness that Muhammad is his servant and messenger.'

You can state this phrase in privacy by yourself or in public with witnesses, which is recommended. You will have help with the accuracy of the pronunciation of the wording in Arabic. The testimony of faith is recommended and often done publicly, in a Mosque or gathering.

13

You testify, acknowledge, and avow you are convinced that no deity is worthy of worship and veneration other than Allah. Allah is the unique name of God, the ultimate Creator. You acknowledge that there is only one God, the Sustainer, the Creator, who controls all matters and all things and has no partners, children, or associates. He is the Most-High, Most-Merciful, All-Knowing, All-Wise, All-Seeing, All-Hearing; he is the First; He is the Last.

You also testify and acknowledge that Muhammad, peace and blessings be upon him, is God's last and final messenger, sent to relay the same general Message as the prophets before him. He is the best example and role model for humanity, a slave and worshipper of Allah, and should not be wrongly worshipped like past Prophets—who were only human messengers of God and not God himself.

FOR THOSE THAT ARE UNSURE
IF THEY SHOULD CONVERT

If you are still unsure whether to convert to Islam, you can pray to God without explicitly naming him, praying out and saying, *Oh you who created me, please guide me to the truth.* Then continue to research and look further into the overwhelming evidence and proof that Islam and the Holy Quran offer to affirm its existence and validity. Do not procrastinate, and do not take this matter of faith lightly, as you are not guaranteed a tomorrow! Your life test can end at any moment. Realize, my dear brother or sister, that you did not come to this randomly or by chance. Your Creator has guided you here.

AFTER YOU CONVERT

Now that you have completed your testimony of faith, you are officially Muslim. As a new convert, you do not need to be burdened by past sins committed before your acceptance, as all your past sins would be wiped clean, and you start with a clean slate— as free of sin as a newborn child. Not only that but all your past sins would be converted to good deeds. You should attempt to the best of your ability to keep your slate clean as much as possible and do as many good deeds as you can. As a new convert, you will make a lot of supplications to God, asking him to continue to guide you on the straight path and lead you to Paradise and everything else you desire—in this world and the Hereafter.

You gradually continue to learn more about Islam and practice it by performing your five mandatory ritualized prayers that all Muslims perform daily. You should not try to learn all aspects of the faith at once, as that might overwhelm you. Instead, continue to learn and grow your new faith over an extended period. This is a life journey, so don't try to do everything at once; but at the same time, don't take it lightly. It's highly recommended to find a local mosque or Islamic community, attend their gatherings, seek support, and make new friends. You should also give charity and fast during Ramadan, which is mandatory for every Muslim.

WHAT YOU NEED
TO BELIEVE IN

Now that you have converted to the fold, you must believe in the six Articles of Iman (Faith). These six articles of Faith form the foundation of the Islamic belief system. Linguistically, the Arabic term "Iman," which translates to "Faith," comes from a root word that means "to give safety and security." Iman makes one feel safe and secure. Without Faith, you would fall into a state of despair. The root word of Iman means to believe in the truth of something or someone, imbuing you with a genuine sense of peace. You must accept God's tenets and teachings, verbalize those concepts with your tongue, and manifest God's teachings in your actions. Believing in and relying upon God will lead you to find safety, security, and contentment even in times of hardship. You acknowledge that you are not alone. God is always with you and fully knows of your situation.

You are asked to believe in what you have never seen with your own eyes, which is the essence of Faith itself. Belief in God is natural for humans. Humans, by nature, are believers in God, as belief in God is inherent in them.

"Indeed, those who fear their Lord unseen will have forgiveness and a great reward." (Quran 67:12)

The six articles of Faith:

BELIEF IN THE ONENESS
OF ALLAH

The first article of faith in Islam is the belief in the Oneness of God. Faith begins with believing in Allah, the Glorious, from which all other facets of Faith spring. You must adhere to and acknowledge that no deity is worthy of your worship, love, subservience, hope, and fear other than Allah. Nothing in existence is worthy of your ultimate loyalty and sacrifice nor worth lowering your head in prostration or humility, except for Allah, the Creator of All.

Islam is monotheistic, believing that there is only One God and He is the only One worthy of worship. The idea of multiple gods is rejected in Islam, as is highlighted many times throughout the Qur'an.

"They have certainly disbelieved who say, 'Allah is the third of three,' And there is no god except one God. And if they do not desist from what they are saying, there will surely afflict the disbelievers among them a painful punishment." (Quran 5:73)

The most severe sin in Islam is known as shirk, which translates to the concept of ascribing a partner to Allah. The term also encompasses attributing divine qualities to any other besides Allah. Shirk is the only sin that God does not forgive if a person dies before repenting.

The Christian belief that Jesus is the son of God, or God himself, is an example of shirk. The belief in the concept of the Trinity— the father, son, and holy spirit—is a grave sin in Islam. Allah states in the Holy Quran that on the Day of Judgment, Prophet Jesus, peace be upon him, will deny ever asking people to worship him instead of God or along with God:

"And remember when Allah will say on the Day of Resurrection: 'O 'Jesus, son of Mary! Did you say unto men: 'Worship me and my mother as two gods besides Allah?' 'He will say: 'Glory be to You! It was not for me to say what I had no right to say. Had I said such a thing, You would surely have known it. You know what is in my inner-self though I do not know what is in Yours, truly, You, only You, are the All-Knower of all that is hidden and unseen." (Quran 5:116)

God is the One to whom worship is due. He is the Creator, Provider, and Sustainer of everything. He is the Supreme, the Eternal. God has no father nor mother, no son or daughter, no partner nor equal. He is All-Knowing, All-Seeing, All-Hearing, All-Powerful, and Most-Merciful. It is He who gives life and causes death. It is He who is Unique in His Names and Attributes.

Everything in this world and everything it contains, the whole universe, including you and me, belong to the One God. We use the phrases "my hand," "my house," and "my money," but it all belongs to God.

"To Allah belongs whatever is in the heavens and whatever is in the Earth. Whether you show what is within yourselves or conceal it, Allah will bring you to account for it. Then He will forgive whom He wills and punish whom He wills, and Allah is over all things competent." (Quran 2:284)

BELIEF IN

THE ANGELS OF ALLAH

The second article of faith to embrace is the belief in the Angels. The Angels are part of the unseen world; we cannot comprehend and prove it scientifically. You cannot see the Angels unless God allows you to and enables your vision. Muslims believe in Angels because they are mentioned numerous times throughout the Holy Quran and in the sayings of the Prophet Muhammad, peace be upon him, a body of work that Muslims call Hadith.

"The Messenger has believed in what was revealed to him from his Lord, and so have the believers. All of them have believed in Allah and His Angels and His Books and His Messengers..."
(Quran 2:285)

God describes Angels' appearance, attributes, characteristics, and responsibilities in His Holy Book. We do not know precisely when the Angels were created, but they predate the creation of human beings. The Angels were created from pure shining light (Noor in Arabic). They are light-giving entities. Angels are generally more powerful than humans and travel at the speed of light. The Angels have certain specialties and capacities that humans do not possess. God refers to the Angels as honored servants.

"...Rather, they are but honored servants." (Quran 21:26)

In Arabic, Angels are called 'Mala'ika,' which means "to assist and help." Angels are Holy and exist in a constant state of worship and praise to God all day and all night; they do not disobey Him. They worship Allah constantly without growing bored or tired.

"They exalt Him night and day and do not slacken."
(Quran 21:20)

The sole purpose of the Angels is to execute the commandments of Allah. An Angel has no needs or desires for material goods. Angels do not eat, drink, sleep, marry, or procreate. The Angels do not die. The same Angels that existed when Prophet Adam, peace be upon him, was created still exist today and will continue to live until the trumpet is blown for the Day of Judgment.

"...And none knows the soldiers of your Lord except Him..."
(Quran 74:31)

The Angels have no gender; they are not female nor male. Angels are physically very beautiful, except the Angel guardian of the hellfire, who wears a stern expression and never laughs. The Greatest of these Angels are magnificent in size, far beyond our imagination. The largest and most significant is the Angel Gabriel (Jibril in Arabic), the Angel descended from Heavens to instruct the Prophets on how to teach and preach the religion. All Angels have wings; some possess two, three, or four pairs - or more. Angel Gabriel has 600 wings and is of a size so great that it fills the space between Heaven and Earth, blocking the entire horizon.

You learn about the Angels to ponder, reflect, and reaffirm the Greatness of your Creator. The experience of having knowledge and belief in the Angels adds to the awe you feel toward God, in that He can create this great being and, indeed, can create whatever He Pleases and Wills. The awe and magnificence of the Almighty's creation reveal and indicate the Magnificence, Glory, and Majesty of the Almighty Himself. This should humble you and increase your God-consciousness, love, and fear of the Almighty. Knowing of the Angels also reminds you that your actions are continuously recorded by the Angels, hopefully decreasing your sins and increasing your good deeds.

BELIEF IN THE BOOKS

OF ALLAH

You are obligated to believe in all inspired Books that God has sent to humanity, as delivered through His Prophets. Every Prophet received Inspiration from God. The Arabic word for Inspiration or Revelation is "Wahi" which has several meanings. Wahi means an idea or something revealed or written, commandment, suggestion, to point out something, or to send a message. Inspiration or Revelation comes to God's Human Prophets directly or through an intermediary of the Angel, Gabriel, who brings Revelation to them.

God's Books contain His Speech, His Message to you and to humanity, which include His commandments, prohibitions, exhortations, stories, parables, reminders, descriptions of Himself and His Attributes, descriptions of the afterlife, Heaven and Hell, the purpose of life, the creation of the Universe, Worship, Piety, morals, manners, the importance of being kind to one's parents, and much more.

These Books seek to guide you through every aspect of your life. God's Books act as a guide, an instructional manual on how to live your life. God, in a high manifestation of His Mercy, Compassion, and Love, sent Books to teach and guide humanity.

"...Your Lord is the possessor of vast Mercy..." (Qur'an 6:147)

Islam counts as an article of faith, the belief in all of God's Books in their original, pure form.

"Say, [O believers], 'We have believed in Allah and what has been revealed to us and what has been revealed to Abraham and Ishmael and Isaac and Jacob and the Descendants and what was given to Moses and Jesus and what was given to the prophets from their Lord. We make no distinction between any of them, and we are Muslims [in submission] to Him.'" (Quran 2:136)

The Old and New Testaments present today are not the Revelations sent with Prophet Moses and Prophet Jesus, peace be upon them. The present-day Old and New Testaments have been altered by men and contain mixtures of human-made ideas and innovations that have corrupted their current state. Whereas these Books may still contain some remaining traces of truth, they do not stand in their original revealed form. God warns in his final Testament, the Holy Quran:

"So, woe to those who write the 'scripture' with their own hands, then say,' This is from Allah,' to exchange it for a small price. Woe to them for what their hands have written and woe to them for what they earn." (Quran 2:79)

When previous Holy Scriptures were altered and corrupted by human hands, God in his Mercy, enlisted his last Revelation, the Holy Quran. God has taken it upon Himself to safeguard and protect his final Book to humanity from human-made alterations or corruption.

The Holy Quran is the only scripture in its original language and words today. Not one letter of the Holy Quran has been changed since its Revelation. The Holy Quran is meant to serve and teach all people until the end of time. Everything in the Holy Quran is truth, with no evidence of contradictions or falseness, and it will remain so for eternity.

Muslims believe that the Holy Quran abrogates all previous Scriptures before it, meaning it cancels the rulings of earlier scriptures and renders them inapplicable going forward since the preceding scriptures were meant for earlier nations and not for us.

In his infinite wisdom, God did not feel fit to send down the Holy Quran for previous nations. As the Creator of the World and everything it contains, God knows who would understand and who would not. Although different revelations came down to various Prophets and nations, the general Message had always remained the same: To worship God Alone and to follow his Commandments.

BELIEF IN THE PROPHETS
AND MESSENGERS OF ALLAH

Believing in God's Prophets and Messengers is fundamental to Islam. God sent Prophets and Messengers to convey his Message to humanity. The Holy Quran states:

"And We certainly sent into every nation a messenger, saying, 'Worship Allah and avoid Ta'ghut (false deities).' And among them were those whom Allah guided, and among them were those upon whom error was [deservedly] decreed. So, proceed through the Earth and observe how was the end of the deniers."
(Quran 16:36)

Every people, every nation, was given a Prophet; they were sent with the tongue of the people. God communicates His guidance through human Prophets. These Prophets were sent to guide people, not only by preaching to worship the One God and follow His commandment, but they set an example with their actions. The Islamic Tradition states that about 124,000 Prophets were sent to people and nations and 310 odd Messengers. There are 25 Prophets mentioned by name in the Holy Quran. Muslims believe all Prophets and Messengers were mere human beings, not divine or semi-divine. They do not have the right to be worshipped, adored, revered, venerated, nor did they claim so.

BELIEF IN THE LAST DAY, RESURRECTION, AND JUDGMENT DAY

"Then when the Horn is blown with one blast, And the Earth and the mountains are lifted and leveled with one blow, Then on that Day, the Resurrection will occur." (Quran 69:13-15)

The fifth pillar of faith is the belief that there will be a last day on this Earth, you will be resurrected and judged in front of God the Almighty, the ultimate Judge, based on your intentions and deeds. You would either go to Paradise or Hellfire.

BELIEF IN DIVINE PREDESTINATION

T he last pillar of the Islamic faith that you must believe in is the concept of Divine Decree. When you believe in this tenet, you affirm that everything - good or bad - that happens in your life emanates from God, the Almighty, and is something He wills to happen. The Arabic word for Divine Decree is Al-Qadr, which translates to measure, determine, assess, decide, and judge. In the context of religion, the term means "Divine determined measurements and sustenance for everyone and everything, by His Wisdom and Power." God states in his Book:

"Indeed, all things We created with predestination."
(Quran 54:49)

God the Almighty, being All-Knowing and All-Wise, knows what we have done in the past, what we are doing now, and what we will do in the future— even before birth. After all, can God be God if He doesn't know everything, including the future? Whereas humanity has the free will to make their own choices, everything happens only and directly through God's Will and Power.

If you question why you are held responsible for the choices and actions you make if God decreed all of them before your birth, you must realize that whatever has been written about you was written only because you will make those choices on your own. You would not be making choices in life because they were written beforehand. They were written beforehand because God can foretell the future, and He decided to write everything that will happen until the day of Judgment on a tablet.

But because God wrote all that will occur in your life on a tablet doesn't mean that God determined or dictated the choices and actions you will take and that these decisions were preordained against your will. God wrote all your actions because you will commit them; you did not commit them because God wrote them. Everyone has the free will to make whatever choice they want.

What You Need
to Practice

Islam is based on five primary foundations or Pillars. Just as a building would lack stability without solid pillars, your relationship with God will lack focus and a secure connection without the observance of and adherence to these five fundamental Pillars. These Five Pillars or religious duties are mandatory; you must follow and enact them with utmost devotion. Failure to comply and enact any of these dictates can lead to the commission of grave sins, some resulting in the expulsion of a believer from the fold and faith of Islam.

Like the Ten Commandments, these Pillars provide a spiritual foundation and framework to facilitate your life. Fulfilling these Five Pillars provides blessings and rewards for you in this life and the next. These Pillars help you establish a closer relationship with your Creator and build a spiritual connection with Him. You must prioritize these Pillars over all worldly matters, principles, or regulations in your life, as they form the foundation and starting point for all other good deeds and acts of worship to your Creator. These Five Pillars are mentioned individually throughout the Holy Quran, and through narrations of Prophet Muhammad, peace be upon him, known as Hadith. The Five Pillars of Islam are:

Testimony of faith in the Oneness of God Allah and the last and final Prophet, Muhammad, Peace be upon him

The first pillar, the declaration and testimony of faith, ranks as the first of the vital, integral Pillars. The remaining principles relate to putting faith into action, as you must apply your faith in behavior and practice. The other four Pillars are religious acts to be performed either daily, once a year, or at least once in a lifetime toward the attainment and accomplishment of faith.

The word Shahada in Arabic linguistically translates to mean "testifying, bearing witness." The Shahada is the Islamic creed. The Shahada contains two parts that a Muslim must testify to and believe. The first part requires the believer to testify that no deity is worthy of worship, veneration, or complete devotion other than Allah. A Muslim acknowledges that Allah has the exclusive right to be worshipped, venerated, loved inwardly and outwardly by one's heart, tongue, and limbs.

Regretfully, many have regarded certain historical figures as their gods and deities, who are wrongfully worshipped and venerated, whether idols, superstitions, saints, ideologies, ways of life, or any authority figures who claim to be divine or semi-divine--even though they are creations with no power to bring any benefit or harm to anyone.

"But they have taken besides Him gods which create nothing, while they are created, and possess not for themselves any harm or benefit and possess not power to cause death or life or resurrection." (Quran 25:3)

One enters the fold of Islam by verbally stating these words, believing in them, acting on them, and living upon them. Merely saying these words verbally, without accompanying action, does not complete a Muslim.

The second part of the testimony requires you to testify that Prophet Muhammad, peace be upon him, is the Messenger of God. In accepting Prophet Muhammad PBUH as the "seal of the Prophets," you affirm that his Prophecy confirms and fulfills all previously revealed Messages beginning with those delivered by Prophet Adam, peace be upon him. You carry out the instruction given by Prophet Muhammad, PBUH--as commanded by God the Almighty. Prophet Muhammad, PBUH, also serves as the best role model for humanity, one who proves his worth through his exemplary life. Muslims are encouraged to follow and emulate Prophet Muhammad PBUH's examples, manners, generosity, good habits, politeness, respect, gentleness, noble feelings, and way of life to the best of their ability, with an emphasis on Islam and the Holy Quran.

"There has certainly been for you in the Messenger of Allah an excellent pattern for anyone whose hope is in Allah and the Last Day and who remembers Allah often." (Quran 33:21)

These two phrases are the most frequently repeated words worldwide, as hundreds of millions of practicing Muslims iterate these words dozens of times throughout their day and through their prayers. It is recommended for a believer to recite them when they first rise in the morning and before going to bed. These words reflect and encompass every dimension of a Muslim's life.

The Shahada (testimony of faith) is by far the essential aspect of Islam, as it affirms the belief in the Oneness and Uniqueness of Allah upon which the whole Religion of Islam is built, and all other beliefs hinge. It is the central belief that a Muslim adheres to for his entire life. Verbally stating these words and living by them is unquestionably a Muslim's most significant and most important duty. Unless you acknowledge this testimony, you cannot be a Muslim.

Muslims strain to utter these words as their last spoken before departing this world since whoever does so has been promised the destiny of God-given Paradise. However, only the ones who lived and acted upon these words will be granted the ability to utter these blessed sentiments in the form of their final words.

ESTABLISHMENT OF
THE FIVE MANDATORY PRAYERS

The second Pillar of Islam is the mandatory round of ritual prayers that must be performed five times daily. The Islamic method of prayer is a ritualized form of worship, which involves the recitation of Verses from the Holy Quran and supplications to God, all while standing, bowing, and prostrating. This mandatory act of worship is called Salah in Arabic and differs from merely praying or supplicating to God in an impulsive act, i.e., just speaking one's mind. Instead, the Salah prayers demand a formalized structure in which one prays a certain way at specific times, as demonstrated by Prophet Muhammad, peace be upon him, drawing direct inspiration from Angel Gabriel, who learned from God Himself.

The Arabic word Salah, generally translated to mean prayer in English, is linguistically derived from the Arabic word meaning "connection." This mode of prayer connects the servant with his Creator. Salah is your way of establishing direct contact with God the Almighty. Salah represents the affirmation of servanthood and submission to your Creator's Will. In Salah, you acknowledge your weakness and neediness by seeking and begging for God's guidance, mercy, grace, and forgiveness.

Salah, the Islamic ritualized prayer, is one form of worship amongst many in this beautiful faith. However, Salah holds a special status in Islam because the act of prayer builds a relationship between you as a servant and your Creator. Salah is considered the center pole of the Religion of Islam; whoever demolishes or denies this practice in their life also demolishes their religion. According to Islamic Scholars, this is the only form of worship that—if neglected—would exclude the disobedient from the folds of Islam.

When prayer time arrives, you are expected to discontinue your current activity and pray to connect with God, the Most Merciful, thereby refreshing your faith for your benefit. Prayer helps remind you as to why you are here and for what purpose. Prayers help direct your thoughts and actions away from sin, from that which is not beneficial. Prayers redirect your thoughts to the remembrance of God.

God commands you to establish and perfect your prayer by praying properly with concentration and the utmost humility. You must work and practice to improve your prayer technique, which takes a lifetime commitment. You must engage in a lifelong effort to master this art of communication with your Creator. The ones who fall into a habitual routine of reciting their words without concentration and humility will miss the objective of prayer, thus not benefitting from their prayer as deeply as those who pray earnestly and with full concentration and mindfulness.

Neglecting mandatory prayer is a grave sin in the Islamic faith. Allah, the glorious, shares a dialogue in the Holy Quran in which the residents of Paradise ask the people condemned to hellfire the reason for their condemnation, and the condemned respond:

"They will say, 'We were not of those who prayed, nor did we used to feed the poor, and we used to indulge in vain talk with the vain talkers, and we used to deny the Day of Recompense, Until there came to us the certainty'" (Quran 74:43-47)

The state of your Prayer record will be the first thing asked of each of us on the Great Day of Judgement. If your prayers are in order, then everything else will fall into place. If your Prayers are not in order, then you will be doomed. The Messenger of Allah stated: *The first of man's deeds for which he will be called to account on the Day of Resurrection will be Salat. If it is found to be perfect, he will be safe and successful; but if it is incomplete, he will be unfortunate and a loser.... (At-Tirmidhi).*

Prayer should be directed only to God the Almighty, as he is the Only One in complete control of everything—including man's destiny. He is All-Powerful, All-Wise, All-Knowing, and All-Hearing, can fill anyone's needs, and remove all of man's pain and miseries.

The Islamic prayer ritual expresses submission to God, showing humility, as well as the ultimate devotion toward and love of God. Praying to the Creator daily is the best way to build a personal connection with Him while seeking His guidance, Blessings, and Forgiveness. You must pray to God to gain spiritual strength and peace of mind and to strengthen your faith's foundation. You must take a break from your daily activities five times a day to connect to God - to stay mindful of Him in this world of stress, struggle, and distractions. The ritual of prayer reminds Muslims that Allah controls all things, a realization that allows you to put your worldly concerns into perspective.

The Islamic prayer method and mode act as a spiritual diet. Just as the body requires food and water throughout the day, your spirit needs to partake in the remembrance and worship of God to stay spiritually healthy. Is not the soul more valuable than the body?

When someone does you a favor or helps you, it's human nature to want to thank that individual for their aid. Since God has blessed you with countless favors, including your wealth, health, family, and gifts of all kinds, you must pray numerous times to thank Him throughout your day and night. The best way to demonstrate gratitude is through the five daily prayers.

Concern and Almsgiving
to the Needy (Zakat)

Zakat is the third pillar of Islam. Zakat translates to mean "the act of giving alms to the poor and needy." Offering Zakat is a religious obligation for Muslims. In Islam, it is considered the duty of individuals of wealth to assist the poor and needy. The term Zakat in Arabic linguistically carries several meanings, including "to purify, to increase, cleanliness, blessings, and goodness."

Zakat means to purify. According to the Islamic faith, your wealth and property are not pure unless you share a divinely appointed proportion of your earnings with people in need. The principle of Zakat also purifies your heart of greed and selfishness. Whereas the humanistic love of wealth is natural, Zakat is intended to free you from the excessive and all-consuming love of money and selfish desire, thereby teaching you self-discipline.

"Take, [O, Muhammad], from their wealth a charity by which you purify them and cause them increase and invoke Allah's blessings upon them. Indeed, your invocations are reassurance for them. And Allah is Hearing and Knowing." (Quran 9:103)

Zakat also translates to mean growth and blessings. If you give and help others in times of ease and difficulties, God will be pleased, increasing and blessing your wealth in response. Allah, the Glorious, has promised that if you spend your wealth in Zakat, your prosperity will increase manifold.

"The example of those who spend their wealth in the way of Allah is like a seed of grain which grows seven spikes; in each spike is a hundred grains. And Allah multiplies His reward for whom He wills. And Allah is all-Encompassing and Knowing."
(Quran 2:261)

Our Prophet has stated that the act of Charity does not decrease wealth; instead, this act blesses, purifies, and ultimately increases one's fortune. Islam requires you to pay an annual contribution of 2.5 percent of the wealth and liquid assets you have accrued over one lunar year. Your personal Zakat is calculated on your earned net balance; that amount remaining after paying all other necessary expenses. Zakat is not an income tax; the amount due is based on what you have saved and held for an entire year. Zakat is not paid from the funds needed for debt repayment or necessary living expenses such as food, water, shelter, clothing, and transportation.

It's important to note that Zakat money needs to be given from an untainted pool of 100% pure and halal funds—not taken from thefts or bribes, nor profits from interest-based loans or sales of alcohol, pork, drugs, or anything prohibited in Islam. God, the Almighty, is Good and Pure and accepts only that which is good and pure.

FASTING DURING T HE MONTH OF RAMADAN (FOR SELF-PURIFICATION)

Fasting during the Month of Ramadan is the 4th pillar of Islam. The Holy Month of Ramadan is the ninth month of the Islamic lunar calendar and can last 29 or 30 days. Muslims fast by abstaining from eating, drinking, chewing gum, smoking, and partaking in any sexual activity from dawn to sunset. Fasting in Islam does not consist solely of refraining from food and drink; instead, you abstain from evil, selfish desire, and wrongdoing. The purpose of fasting is not merely for the body; instead, it's for the spirit as well.

Fasting during Ramadan is for the benefit of your soul, mind, and body. You are commanded to refrain from gossiping, backbiting, slandering, lying, cheating, looking at material that is prohibited, nursing a grudge, using sinful speech, and any wrongdoing. You must adhere to the morals of Islam strictly during your fast, as failure to do so can violate your fast.

Fasting during Ramadan is obligatory for every sane, healthy Muslim who is not ill nor traveling long distances, whether male or female, unless a female is on her menstruation cycle or experiencing post-childbirth bleeding. The primary reason Muslims fast is that God the Almighty has commanded us to do so in His Last and Final Revelation, the Holy Quran.

"O, you who believe! Fasting is prescribed to you as it was prescribed to those before you, that ye may become righteous and (hopefully learn) self-restraint." (Quran 2:183)

Fasting is an act of worship beloved by God. The Holy Month of Ramadan and the prescribed fasting is a gift and mercy to you sent directly from the Almighty. God prescribes no rulings to his slaves unless they come complete with great wisdom and benefit. God, the Almighty, states the act of fasting and abstaining from what is prohibited will increase your Taqwa (God-fearing piety, righteousness, mindfulness, and consciousness of God, where you are aware God is always watching). Fasting develops spiritual endurance and self-restraint, helping you control your anger, words, and actions. Fasting helps one to resist unlawful desires and wicked habits, which in turn serves to guard against evil. Fasting during Ramadan suppresses worldly desires and strengthens one's spirituality.

The Holy Month of Ramadan is special and blessed because the Holy Quran, God's final Book, was revealed to Prophet Muhammad, peace be up him, in this special month. Therefore, Muslims recite the Holy Quran frequently in this blessed month. During Ramadan, Muslims try to establish or re-establish a relationship with their Creator and the Holy Quran so they may be guided down the right path. Ramadan is a month for deep inner reflection.

THE PILGRIMAGE

TO MAKKAH

Image: T

he fifth pillar of Islam is Hajj, which translates to mean "the pilgrimage to the Holy city of Makkah." The Arabic word, Hajj, linguistically, means "heading to a place for the sake of visiting." In Islamic terminology, the term describes the act of heading to Makkah to observe specific actions and rituals. Hajj, or the pilgrimage, is a 5-6-day journey to this sacred place between the 8th and 13th day of the last month of the Islamic lunar calendar, Dhul-Hijjah. The Hajj journey is obligatory for every Muslim, male or female, to complete at least once in a lifetime, provided they are mentally, physically, and financially capable of making the trip. God states:

"...And due to Allah from the people is a pilgrimage to the House - for whoever is able to find thereto a way..." (Quran 3:97)

The Hajj includes detailed reenactments of certain symbolic rituals performed by great Prophets and righteous individuals in the past. The Hajj Pilgrimage and its symbolic rituals commemorate the legacy of Prophet Abraham, peace be upon him; this is why one needs to learn about Prophet Abraham to understand the reasoning behind individual acts performed as a part of Hajj.

Integral to Hajj is the Kaaba, a holy shrine - a black silk-clad cube stone structure at the heart of the Grand Mosque in the modern-day city of Mecca, Saudi Arabia. The Kaaba is at the center of the Earth, built by Prophet Abraham and his son Ismael, peace be upon them. Upon completion, God the Almighty commanded Prophet Abraham to relay a single Message to the people: that they would be required to make a pilgrimage to this House.

May your journey to the answer
and the truth be pleasant and successful.

The Sincere Seeker's Introductory book to Islam,

'*The Sacred Path to Islam*,' and other Islamic books for adults and children
are available on The Sincere Seeker's Amazon
page: www.amazon.com/thesincereseeker

You are encouraged to visit and subscribe to
The Sincere Seeker's Blog at www.TheSincereSeeker.com and

The Sincere Seeker's YouTube
Channel: www.YouTube.com/c/TheSincereSeeker

For questions or comments, please contact me
at: hello@thesincereseeker.com

Ready to submit to your Creator?

You can convert to Islam and become
Muslim in a 5-min Call with me. Schedule your call here:

https://www.thesincereseeker.com/
convert-to-islam-and-become-muslim/

Made in the USA
Coppell, TX
19 November 2024